Try Not to Laugh Challenge
Challenge

CHRISTMAS
Joke Book for Kids

A Hilarious and Interactive Holiday Themed Game Book for Ages 7-13

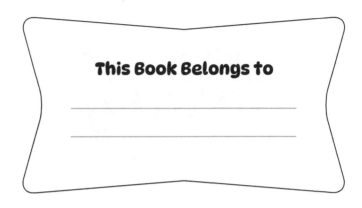

This Book Belongs to

_____

_____

Thanks!

Thank you for your purchase. If you enjoyed this book, please consider dropping us a review. It takes only 5 seconds and helps small independent publishers like ours.

TRY NOT TO LAUGH CHALLENGE: CHRISTMAS JOKES FOR KIDS

Spot illustrations: Creative Fabrica & Freepik.com

Contents

Try Not to Laugh Challenge
Rules

Two players face off against each other for three rounds. (A round consists of one joke.) One of the players is the "jester" and has to try to make the other player laugh by reading jokes from the book. The "straight man" is the player who has to try not to smile or laugh, no matter what the "jester" reads. If the straight man laughs, the jester gets the point. If the straight man doesn't laugh, the straight man gets the point. The person with the most points after three rounds wins!

We recommend having a time limit for your challenges. If you can't get another person to laugh in 1-2 minutes, the challenge is over, and it's time for someone else to try!

Have fun!

v

1

Santa Snickers

Why don't you ever see Santa in the hospital?

Because he has private elf care!

How do you know when Santa's around?

You can always sense his presents!

Where does Santa keep all his money?

At the local snow bank!

What do you call a broke Santa?

Saint Nickel-less!

What do you call Santa when he takes a break?

Santa Pause!

What did Santa say to the smoker?

"Please don't smoke, it's bad for my elf!"

What kind of motorcycle does Santa like to ride?

A Holly Davidson!

What do you get when Santa becomes a detective?

Santa Clues!

What does Mrs! Claus say to Santa when there are clouds in the sky?

"It looks like rain, deer!"

What does Santa suffer from if he gets stuck in a chimney?

Claus-trophobia!

Who delivers presents to baby sharks at Christmas?

Santa Jaws!

What do you call a kid who doesn't believe in Santa?

A rebel without a Claus!

Knock, knock!

Who's there?

Claus!

Claus who?

Claus I can't wait any longer!

What goes "Oh, Oh, Oh"?

Santa walking backwards!

Why does Santa have three gardens?

So he can 'ho ho ho'!

How much did Santa pay for his sleigh?

Nothing!
It was on the house!

What nationality is Santa Claus?

North Polish!

Why does Santa Claus go down the chimney on Christmas Eve?

Because it soot's him!

What is Santa Claus' laundry detergent of choice?

Yule-Tide!

How does Santa keep his
bathroom tiles immaculate?

He uses Comet!

What do you say to Santa
when he's taking
attendance at school?

"Present!"

What do you get if Santa
goes down the chimney
when a fire is lit?

Crisp Kringle!

What's as big as Santa but weighs nothing?

Santa's shadow!

Where does Santa always stay when he goes on any vacation?

At the ho-ho-ho-tel!

What does Santa do when the reindeer drive too fast?

Hold on for deer life!

Knock, knock!

Who's there?

Dexter!

Dexter who?

Dexter halls with boughs of holly!!!

What does Santa say when he gets sick?

"Oh oh no!"

What's red, white, and green?

Santa Claus when he's travel sick!

How does Santa take photos?

With a Pole-aroid camera, of course!

How does Santa Claus keep
track of every fireplace he
has already visited?

Well, he keeps a log!

What is Santa's favorite
place to deliver presents?

Idaho-ho-ho!

Did you hear that Santa
knows karate?

He has a black belt!

How do you wash your hands over the holidays?

With Santa-tizer!

What's the difference between Santa Clause and a knight?

One slays a dragon,
the other drags a sleigh!

What was Santa's favorite subject in school?

Chemis-tree!

What smells most in a chimney?

Santa's nose!

What did Santa say at the start of the race?

Ready, set, ho ho ho!

What do you get if Santa forgets to wear his underclothes?

Saint Knicker-less!

Knock, knock!

Who's there?

Ima!

Ima who?

Ima dreaming of a white Christmas!!!

What did the ocean say to Santa?

Nothing, it just waved!

What's red, white and spotty?

Santa Claus with chickenpox!

Where does Santa go swimming?

The North Pool!

2
Raucous Reindeer

What do you call an obnoxious reindeer?

Rude-olph!

What do reindeers say before they tell you a joke?

"This one's gonna sleigh you!"

How does Rudolph know when Christmas is coming?

He refers to his calen-deer!

Why didn't Rudolph get a good report card?

Because he went down in history!

What do you call a blind reindeer?

I have no eye deer!

Why are Comet, Cupid, and Donner always wet?

Because they are rain deer!

How did the reindeer know it was going to rain?

Because Rudolph the red-knows-rain, deer!

Which one of Santa's reindeer has the best moves?

Dancer!

What's worse than a reindeer with a runny nose?

A snowman with a fever!

Where do Santa's reindeer stop for coffee?

Star-bucks!

Why don't reindeer like picnics?

Because of all their ant-lers!

What did Rudolph have to say about a big book of noses that Santa gifted him?

He said,
"I already red that one!"

Knock, knock!

Who's there?

Olive!

Olive who?

Olive the other reindeer used to laugh and call him names...

What do you call a scary looking reindeer?

A cari-boo!

What do reindeer hang on their Christmas trees?

Horn-aments!

Why do Donner and Blitzen get to take so many coffee breaks?

Because they are Santa's star bucks!

Did Rudolph the red nosed reindeer go to school?

No, he was elf-taught!

What's got four legs and flashes red?

Rudolph needing his nose changed!

What did the reindeer say to the elf?

Nothing!!!
Reindeer can't talk!

Why did the red-nosed reindeer help the old lady cross the road?

It would have been Rudolph him not to!

What does a reindeer do when he has an upset stomach?

He takes an elk-a-seltzer!

What does Rudolph want for Christmas?

A pony sleigh-station!

3

Exuberant Elves

What do you call an elf that can sing and dance?

Elfis!

What does an elf study in school?

The elf-abet!

What is an elf's favorite sport?

North-pole vaulting!

What kind of photos do elves take?

Elfies!

Why was Santa's little helper depressed?

Because he had very low elf esteem!

Did you know that Santa's not allowed to go down chimneys this year?

It was declared unsafe by the Elf and Safety Commission!

How do you help someone who's lost their Christmas spirit?

Nurse them back to elf!

What do you call an elf wearing ear muffs?

Anything you want, he can't hear you!

When Santa is on the beach what do the elves call him?

Sandy Claus!

**Why does Santa have elves
in his workshop?**

Because the Seven Dwarfs
were busy!

**How long are an
elf's legs?**

Just long enough to
reach the ground!

**Why doesn't Santa
eat junk food?**

Because it's bad for your elf!

Knock, knock!

Who's there?

Elf!

Elf who?

Elf I knock again will you let me in?!

What's every elf's favorite type of music?

Wrap!

What type of cars do the elves of Santa Claus drive?

Toy-otas!

What do elves do after school?

Their gnome-work!

What do you call a greedy elf?

Elf-ish!

What does Santa use to bake cakes?

Elf-raising flour!

What happens to naughty elves?

They get the sack!

What do Santa's elves drive?

Minivans!

What do you call an Elf on the Shelf who just won the lottery?

W-elfy!

What do the elves cook with in the kitchen?

U-tinsels!

Why did the elf put a clock on Santa's sleigh?

He wanted to see time fly!

What kind of money do elves use?

Jingle bills!

What is a typical elf greeting?

"Small world, isn't it?"

4

Ticklish Tree Jokes

What do you get if you eat Christmas decorations?

Tinsil-itis!

What do you get when you combine a Christmas tree with an iPad?

A pine-apple!

How did the ornament get addicted to Christmas?

He was hooked on trees his whole life!

What is a Christmas tree's favorite candy?

Orna-mints!

Why did the Christmas tree go to the barber?

It needed to be trimmed!

What did Mrs! Claus say to Santa when she saw this year's Christmas tree?

You could spruce it up a little!

Why do Christmas trees like the past so much?

Because the present's beneath them!

What did one Christmas tree say to another?

"Lighten up!"

Why are Christmas trees bad at sewing?

Because they always drop their needles!

Who is a Christmas tree's favorite singer?

Spruce Springsteen!

Why did the Christmas tree go to the dentist?

It needed a root canal!

What is a Christmas tree's least favorite month?

Sep-timber!

Knock, knock!

Who's there?

Oh, Chris!

Oh, Chris who?

Oh Christmas tree, Oh Christmas tree...

What part of the body do you only see during Christmas?

Mistle-toe!

What do you call cutting down a Christmas tree?

Christmas chopping!

What did one Christmas light say to the other Christmas light?

"You light me up!"

What did the Christmas tree say to the Christmas ornament?

"Quit hanging around!"

Why wouldn't the Christmas Tree stand?

It had no legs!

How do you decorate a canoe for Christmas?

With oar-naments!

**What did one Christmas tree
decoration say
to the other?**

"Let's hang out!"

**Where does Mistletoe go
to become famous?**

Holly-wood!

**What do you get when
you cross a pine cone
and a polar bear?**

A fur tree!

5

Silly Snowmen

What do snowmen eat for breakfast?

Snowflakes!

How do snowmen get around?

They ride an icicle!

What do snowmen take when the sun gets too hot?

A chill pill!

What does Jack Frost
like best about school?

Snow-and-tell!

What did one snowman say
another snowman?

"You're cool!"

What do snowmen wear
on their heads?

Ice caps!

How do you scare a snowman?

Grab a hairdryer!

Where would you find a snowman dancing?

At a snow-ball!

How does a snowman lose weight?

He waits for the weather to get warmer!

**What song do you sing
at a snowman's birthday party?**

"Freeze a jolly good fellow!"

**What did one snowman say
to the other snowman?**

"Do you smell carrots?"

**What do you call a snowman
with a six-pack?**

The Abdominal Snowman!

Knock, knock!

Who's there?

Snow!

Snow who?

Snow time to waste, Christmas is coming soon!

What do snowmen call
their offspring?

Chill-dren!

Why did Frosty's wife
ask for a divorce?

He was a total flake!

What do snowmen
eat for lunch?

Iceberg-ers!

What's a snowman's favorite food?

Chili!

What do you call an old snowman?

A puddle!

Why does everyone love Frosty the Snowman?

He's cool!

**What happened when the
snow girl broke up with
the snow boy?**

She gave him the cold
shoulder!

**Why did the snowman
turn yellow?**

Ask the little dog over there!

**When is a boat just
like snow?**

When it's a-drift!

Why is winter a snowman's favorite time of year?

Because they can camouflage!

What is it called when a snowman has a temper tantrum?

A meltdown!

What do you get when you cross a snowman with a baker?

Frosty the dough-man!

Knock, knock!

Who's there?

Irish!

Irish who?

Irish you a Merry Christmas!

What two letters of the alphabet do snowmen like best?

"I" and "C"!

Why was the snowman rummaging in the bag of carrots?

He was picking his nose!

Who does Santa call when his sleigh breaks down?

The Abominable Towman!

What did the snowman say to the aggressive carrot?

"Get out of my face!"

How do you lift a frozen car?

With a Jack Frost!

What do snowmen like to do on the weekend?

Just chill!

What kind of ball
doesn't bounce?

A snowball!

What falls at the North Pole
and never gets hurt?

Snow!

What did the snowman say
when he was offered
a hot chocolate?

"Snow, thank you!"

6

Humbug
Hilarity

How did Scrooge win the football game?

The ghost of Christmas Passed!

What does the Grinch do with a baseball bat?

Hits a gnome and runs!

Why does Scrooge love reindeer so much?

Because every single buck is dear to him!

Why do mummies like Christmas so much?

They're into all the wrapping!

What do you get when you cross a snowman with a vampire?

Frostbite!

Why wouldn't Ebenezer Scrooge eat at the pasta restaurant?

It cost a pretty penne!

Why don't aliens celebrate Christmas?

They don't want to give away their presence!

How does Darth Vader enjoy his Christmas Turkey?

On the dark side!

Why does the Grinch hate Christmas?

Because it makes him green with envy!

Knock, knock!

Who's there?

Alaska!

Alaska who?

Alaska again!
What do you want
for Christmas?

7

Christmas
Chuckles

What do you get if you cross Santa with a duck?

A Christmas Quacker!

Where do polar bears vote?

The North Poll!

How does a sheep say Merry Christmas?

"Fleece Navidad!"

How do chickens dance at a Christmas party?

Chick to chick!

What do fish sing during the holidays?

Christmas corals!

What do angry mice send to each other at Christmas?

Cross-mouse cards!

What did the beaver say to the Christmas Tree?

"Nice gnawing you!"

What's the most popular Christmas carol in the desert?

"Oh Caaamel, Ye Faithful!"

What happens when you combine Santa with a duck?

A Christmas Quacker!

What is Santa's dogs name?

Santa Paws!

Why can't penguins fly?

They're not tall enough
to be pilots!

What's green, covered in tinsel, and goes "ribbit, ribbit?"

A Mistle-toad!

Knock, knock!

Who's there?

Donut!

Donut who?

Donut open 'til Christmas!

What would you give a dog as a present for Christmas?

A mobile bone!

How do sheep wish each other happy holidays?

"Merry Christmas to ewe!"

What sort of insects love snow?

Mo-ski-toes!

What kind of pine has the sharpest needles?

A porcu-pine!

Why did the turkey join the band?

Because he had the drum sticks!

What do monkeys sing at Christmas?

Jungle bells!

What happened to the turkey at Christmas?

It got gobbled!

Why did the turkey cross the road?

Because it was the chicken's day off!

What do you get if you cross a bell with a skunk?

Jingle Smells!

**Why wouldn't the cat climb
the Christmas tree?**

It was afraid of the bark!

**What kind of fish do they
have at the North Pole?**

Jolly-fish!

**What bird is the best
at unlocking doors?**

A tur-key!

Knock, knock!

Who's there?

Norway!

Norway who?

Norway am I kissing anyone under the mistletoe!

Which Christmas carol do dogs like best?

"Bark the Herald Angels Sing!"

What do donkeys send out near Christmas?

Mule-tide greetings!

What did the cow say on Christmas morning?

"Mooooey Christmas!"

**Why do cats take so long
to wrap presents?**

They want them to be
purr-fect!

**How do cats greet each
other at Christmas time?**

"A Furry Merry Christmas and
Happy Mew-Year!"

**Which dinosaur loves
Christmas the most?**

Tree-Rex!

8
Festive Food Jokes

Why was the candy cane so expensive?

It was in mint condition!

What does the gingerbread man put on his bed?

Cookie sheets!

Why did the gingerbread man go to the doctor?

He was feeling crummy!

What do Santa's little helpers like to eat on a cold day at the North Pole?

Elf-abet soup!

What's the best thing to put in your Christmas dinner?

Your teeth!

What's Santa's favorite sandwich?

Peanut butter and jolly!

Why should Christmas dinner always be well done?

So you can say
"Merry Crispness!"

What is invisible and smells like milk and cookies?

Santa's burps!

What's red, white, and blue at Christmas time?

A sad candy cane!

What did one cranberry say to another at Christmas?

"'Tis the season to be jelly!"

What's Santa's favorite snack food?

Crisp Pringles!

What is Santa's favorite kind of candy?

Jolly Ranchers!

What do you get when you use a deer-shaped cookie cutter?

Cookie doe!

Who is never hungry at Christmas?

The turkey!
He's always stuffed!

What does Santa eat for breakfast?

Mistle toast!

10

Random Chortles

What's every parent's favorite Christmas Carol?

Silent Night!

Why was the little boy so cold on Christmas morning?

Because it was Decembrrrr!

What comes at the end of Christmas Day?

The letter "Y!"

What happened to the thief who stole a Christmas calendar?

He got 12 months!

What should you give your parents at Christmas?

A list of what you want!

What's red and white and falls down chimneys?

Santa Klutz!

What is the best Christmas present in the world?

A broken drum, you just can't beat it!

What did Adam say the day before Christmas?

"It's Christmas, Eve!"

What would you get if you crossed Christmas with St! Patrick's Day?

St! O'Claus!

**What is the Christmas carol
that you can sing
to fruits?**

"Have Yourself
A Berry Little Christmas!"

**What do you call someone
who can't stop talking about
last Christmas?**

Santa-mental!

**In what year does New Year's
Day come before Christmas?**

Every year!

Knock, knock!

Who's there?

Hannah!

Hannah who?

Hannah partridge in a pear tree!

What's the difference between the Christmas alphabet and the regular alphabet?

The Christmas alphabet has no L!

Why is everyone so thirsty at the North Pole?

No well, no well!

What is the most competitive season?

Win-ter!

What comes at the end of Christmas?

The letter "S!"

What do you call a search engine that sings Christmas songs?

Michael Googlé!

How did Mary and Joseph know Jesus' weight when he was born?

They had a weigh in a manger!

What do you call a bunch of chess players bragging about their games in a hotel lobby?

Chess nuts boasting in an open foyer!

What's a child's favorite king at Christmas?

A stoc-king!

What should you do if your car stalls on Christmas Eve?

You get a mistle-tow!

**Who robs from the rich
so he can gift-wrap presents
for the poor?**

Ribbon Hood!

**What do you call a man who
claps at Christmas?**

Sant-applause!

**When does
Christmas come before
Thanksgiving?**

In the dictionary!

Why didn't the rope get any Christmas presents?

It was knotty!

What did the stamp say to the Christmas card?

"Stick with me and
we'll go places!"

Why is it getting harder to buy Advent calendars?

Their days are numbered!

11

Christmas Puns

Yule be sorry!

I'm s-mitten!

Have a tree-mendous Christmas!

Your presents is requested!

How rude-olf you!

I'm feelin' pine!

Time to spruce things up!

But wait, there's myrrh!

Hold on for deer life!

This is snow laughing matter!

12

Score Cards

Included on the following pages, are score-cards you can use to help keep track of everyone's laughter and determine the ultimate "Try Not to Laugh Challenge" champion. Get ready for some friendly competition and endless laughs as you tally up the scores and crown the funniest person in the room!

Have fun!

Try Not to Laugh Challenge
SCORECARD

After each round, when someone laughs, mark the box with a checkmark or X. Each mark is worth one point. The player with the lowest score wins!

Name	Round 1	Round 2	Round 3	Total
Name	Round 1	Round 2	Round 3	Total
Name	Round 1	Round 2	Round 3	Total
Name	Round 1	Round 2	Round 3	Total
Name	Round 1	Round 2	Round 3	Total

Try Not to Laugh Challenge
SCORECARD

After each round, when someone laughs, mark the box with a checkmark or X. Each mark is worth one point. The player with the lowest score wins!

Name	Round 1	Round 2	Round 3	Total

Name	Round 1	Round 2	Round 3	Total

Name	Round 1	Round 2	Round 3	Total

Name	Round 1	Round 2	Round 3	Total

Name	Round 1	Round 2	Round 3	Total

Try Not to Laugh Challenge
SCORECARD

After each round, when someone laughs, mark the box with a checkmark or X. Each mark is worth one point. The player with the lowest score wins!

Name	Round 1	Round 2	Round 3	Total
Name	Round 1	Round 2	Round 3	Total
Name	Round 1	Round 2	Round 3	Total
Name	Round 1	Round 2	Round 3	Total
Name	Round 1	Round 2	Round 3	Total

Try Not to Laugh Challenge
SCORECARD

After each round, when someone laughs, mark the box with a checkmark or X. Each mark is worth one point. The player with the lowest score wins!

Name	Round 1	Round 2	Round 3	Total

Name	Round 1	Round 2	Round 3	Total

Name	Round 1	Round 2	Round 3	Total

Name	Round 1	Round 2	Round 3	Total

Name	Round 1	Round 2	Round 3	Total

Try Not to Laugh Challenge
SCORECARD

After each round, when someone laughs, mark the box with a checkmark or X. Each mark is worth one point. The player with the lowest score wins!

Name	Round 1	Round 2	Round 3	Total

Name	Round 1	Round 2	Round 3	Total

Name	Round 1	Round 2	Round 3	Total

Name	Round 1	Round 2	Round 3	Total

Name	Round 1	Round 2	Round 3	Total

Made in United States
Cleveland, OH
14 December 2024

11899909R00066